SCHOLASTIC

READ & RESPOND

Helping children discover the pleasure and power of reading

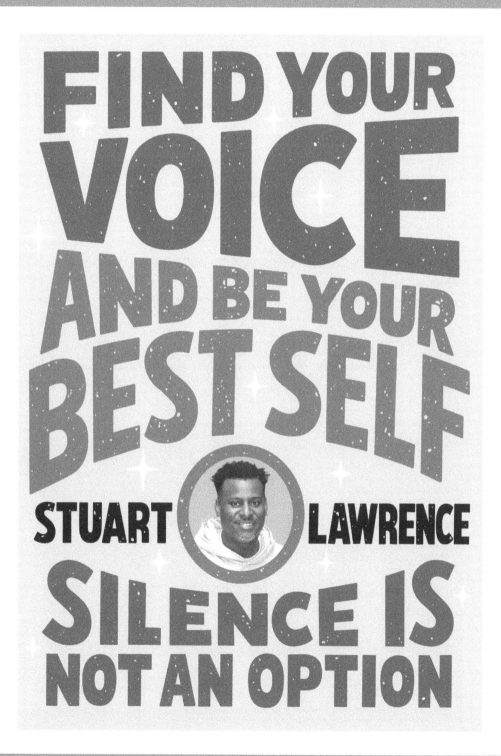

FIND YOUR VOICE AND BE YOUR BEST SELF

STUART LAWRENCE

SILENCE IS NOT AN OPTION

FOR AGES 9–11

Published in the UK by Scholastic, 2022

Scholastic Distribution Centre, Bosworth Avenue, Tournament Fields, Warwick, CV34 6UQ

Scholastic Ireland, 89E Lagan Road, Dublin Industrial Estate, Glasnevin, Dublin, D11 HP5F

SCHOLASTIC and associated logos are trademarks and/or registered trademarks of Scholastic Inc.

www.scholastic.co.uk

© 2022 Scholastic Limited

1 2 3 4 5 6 7 8 9   2 3 4 5 6 7 8 9 0 1

A CIP catalogue record for this book is available from the British Library.
ISBN 978-0702-31947-1

Printed and bound by Ashford Colour Press
The book is made of materials from well-managed,
FSC®-certified forests and other controlled sources.

MIX
Paper from
responsible sources
FSC® C011748

Extracts from *The National Curriculum in England, English Programme of Study* © Crown Copyright. Reproduced under the terms of the Open Government Licence (OGL). http://www.nationalarchives.gov.uk/doc/open-government-licence/version/3

Author Eileen Jones
Editorial team Rachel Morgan, Vicki Yates, Caroline Hale and Helen Cox Cannons
Series designer Andrea Lewis
Typesetter QBS Learning
Illustrator Simone Douglas
Photographs page 30: Nelson Mandela, South Africa The Good News/Wikimedia Commons, John Barnes, Alamy, Stephen Lawrence, Alamy

Acknowledgements
The publishers gratefully acknowledge permission to reproduce the following material:
Scholastic Children's Books for the use of the text extracts and cover from *Silence is Not an Option: Find Your Voice and Be Your Best Self* written by Stuart Lawrence
Every effort has been made to trace copyright holders for the works reproduced in this book, and the publishers apologise for any inadvertent omissions.

For supporting online resources go to:
www.scholastic.co.uk/read-and-respond/books/silence-is-not-an-option/online-resources
Access key: Present

CONTENTS

How to use Read & Respond in your classroom...

Read & Respond provides teaching ideas related to a specific well-loved children's book. Each Read & Respond book is divided into the following sections:

ABOUT THE BOOK AND AUTHOR

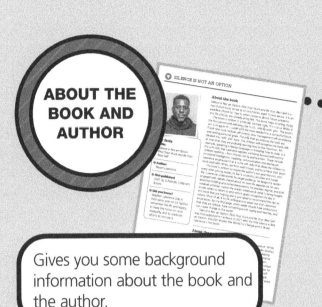

Gives you some background information about the book and the author.

GUIDED READING

Breaks the book down into sections and gives notes for using it, ideal for use with the whole class. A bookmark has been provided on page 12 containing **comprehension** questions. The children can be directed to refer to these as they read. Find comprehensive guided reading sessions on the supporting online resources.

SHARED READING

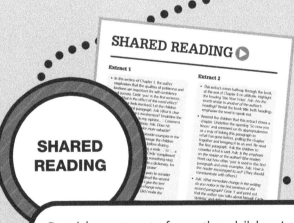

Provides extracts from the children's book with associated notes for focused work. There is also one fiction extract that relates to the children's book.

GRAMMAR, PUNCTUATION & SPELLING

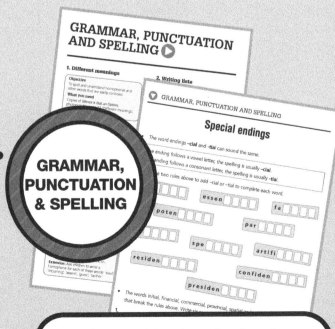

Provides word-level work related to the children's book so you can teach grammar, punctuation, spelling and **vocabulary** in context.

CONTENT & STRUCTURE

Contains activity ideas focused on the content and structure of the book.

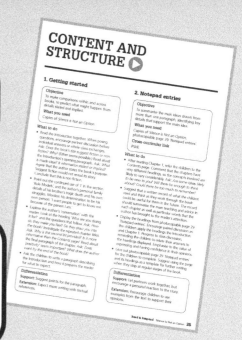

TALK ABOUT IT

Oracy, **fluency**, and speaking and listening activities. These activities may be based directly on the children's book or be broadly based on the themes and concepts of the book.

GET WRITING

Provides writing activities related to the children's book. These activities may be based directly on the children's book or be broadly based on the themes and concepts of the book.

ASSESSMENT

Contains short activities that will help you assess whether the children have understood concepts and curriculum objectives. They are designed to be informal activities to feed into your planning.

SUPPORTING ONLINE RESOURCE

Online you can find a host of supporting documents including planning information, comprehensive guided reading sessions and guidance on teaching reading.

www.scholastic.co.uk/read-and-respond/books/
silence-is-not-an-option/online-resources
Access key: Present

Help children develop a love of **reading for pleasure**.

Activities

The activities follow the same format:

- **Objective:** the objective for the lesson. It will be based upon a curriculum objective, but will often be more specific to the focus being covered.

- **What you need:** a list of resources you need to teach the lesson, including photocopiable pages.

- **What to do:** the activity notes.

- **Differentiation:** this is provided where specific and useful differentiation advice can be given to support and/or extend the learning in the activity. Differentiation by providing additional adult support has not been included as this will be at a teacher's discretion based upon specific children's needs and ability, as well as the availability of support.

The activities are numbered for reference within each section and should move through the text sequentially – so you can use the lesson while you are reading the book. Once you have read the book, most of the activities can be used in any order you wish.

Section	Activity	Curriculum objectives
Guided reading		Comprehension: To predict what might happen from details stated and implied.
Shared reading	1	Comprehension: To read books that are structured in different ways and read for a range of purposes.
	2	Comprehension: To make comparisons within and across books.
	3	Comprehension: To check that the book makes sense to them, discussing their understanding and exploring the meaning of words in context.
	4	Comprehension: To discuss and evaluate how authors use language, including figurative language, considering the impact on the reader.
Grammar, punctuation & spelling	1	Vocabulary, grammar and punctuation: To distinguish between homophones and near homophones.
	2	Vocabulary, grammar and punctuation: To use a colon to introduce a list; To use semicolons…to mark boundaries between independent clauses.
	3	Vocabulary, grammar and punctuation: To understand that words from a text can be useful in their own writing.
	4	Vocabulary, grammar and punctuation: To use hyphens to avoid ambiguity.
	5	Vocabulary, grammar and punctuation: To spell words with endings which sound like /shul/.
	6	Vocabulary, grammar and punctuation: To use modal verbs or adverbs to indicate degrees of possibility.
Content & structure	1	Comprehension: To make comparisons within and across books; To predict what might happen from details stated and implied.
	2	Comprehension: To summarise the main ideas drawn from more than one paragraph, identifying key details that support the main ideas.
	3	Comprehension: To check that the book makes sense to them, exploring the meaning of words in context.
	4	Comprehension: To identify how language, structure and presentation contribute to meaning.
	5	Comprehension: To check that the book makes sense to them… and explaining the meaning of words in context.
	6	Comprehension: To identify and discuss themes and conventions in and across a wide range of writing.
	7	Comprehension: To read books that are structured in different ways and read for a range of purposes.
	8	Comprehension: To provide reasoned justifications for their views.

Section	Activity	Curriculum objectives
Talk about it	1	Spoken language: To give well-structured...narratives for different purposes, including for expressing feelings.
	2	Spoken language: To participate in discussions...and debates.
	3	Spoken language: To use spoken language to develop understanding through speculating, hypothesising, imagining and exploring ideas.
	4	Spoken language: To participate in...role play/improvisations.
	5	Spoken language: To participate in discussions...and debates.
	6	Spoken language: To consider and evaluate different viewpoints, attending to and building on the contribution of others.
Get writing	1	Composition: To draft and write by...précising longer passages.
	2	Composition: To note and develop initial ideas, drawing on reading and research where necessary.
	3	Composition: To plan their writing by identifying the audience for and purpose of the writing.
	4	Composition: To select the appropriate form and use other similar writing as models for their own.
	5	Composition: To plan their writing by noting and developing initial ideas, drawing on reading and research where necessary.
	6	Composition: To assess the effectiveness of their own and others' writing and suggesting improvements.
Assessment	1	Comprehension: To identify how language, structure and presentation contribute to meaning.
	2	Comprehension: To distinguish between statements of fact and opinion.
	3	Comprehension: To retrieve, record and present information from non-fiction.
	4	Composition: To use further organisational and presentational devices to structure text and to guide the reader.
	5	Composition: To select appropriate grammar and vocabulary, understanding how such choices can change and enhance meaning.
	6	Composition: To perform their own compositions, using appropriate intonation, volume and movement so that meaning is clear.

Key facts

◉ **Title:**
Silence is Not an Option: Find Your Voice and Be Your Best Self

◉ **Author:**
Stuart Lawrence

◉ **First published:**
2021 by Scholastic Children's Books

◉ **Did you know?**
Stephen Lawrence Day is held every year on 22 April to remember his life and legacy, to keep the focus on racial inequality and to celebrate efforts to remove it.

About the book

Silence is Not an Option: Find Your Voice and Be Your Best Self is a non-fiction book aimed at schoolchildren aged 10 and above. It is an excellent choice for Year 6, when concerns about future academic and life choices are already being felt. This book helps to bring clarity.

The book is written in a friendly, intimate style. The author writes in the first person and addresses the reader directly with 'you'. The book's aim is to equip the reader with the tools needed for a successful future. These nine tools include self-control, time-management, self-confidence and setting personal goals. The skills that accompany the tools are divided into 'soft' and 'hard'. The children will recognise the hard skills as ones that they are probably learning now in the classroom, for example, speaking a foreign language or knowing how to code. It is the soft skills that Lawrence explains are being learned without the children realising – from friends, family and teachers. These include emotional intelligence, creativity, communication and teamwork. Lawrence emphasises that it is the soft skills that allow the children to work well with others, perform well in tasks and to achieve their goals.

The book is written to inspire the author's ten-year-old son, and every other young reader, to live 'a successful, positive and happy life'. Lawrence understands his target audience: he keeps the reader engaged with details shared about his own life experience; he uses attention-holding and varied presentation; he provides regular, practical notepad activities. Hence the reader understands what is being taught; knows when to return to and rethink goals; recognises the tips in this book that are helping and is prompted to recommend the tips to others. Most of all, it is this willingness to speak out that Lawrence emphasises. By the final page, every reader should have understood that they are unique, have something worth saying and hearing, and can create change in the world.

Silence is Not an Option: Find Your Voice and Be Your Best Self was first published in hardback in 2021 with the title *Silence is Not an Option: You Can Impact the World For Change* and is Stuart Lawrence's first book.

About the author

Stuart Lawrence was born in 1977 and brought up in London. While still a teenager, he suffered a major event in his life: his older brother, Stephen, was killed in a racial attack. The event was a devastating blow for Stuart and he struggled to cope with the loss of a brother whom he regarded as a 'superhero'. He gradually found his own voice, changing courses, recognising the type of learning that suited him, gaining success and working as a teacher for 15 years. Now he is a motivational speaker and youth engagement specialist. He still works within the education system, aiming to equip young people with the mindset to believe that they too can achieve what they want in life, whatever challenges they face.

GUIDED READING ▶

Introduction

Invite the children to examine the book's cover. Consider the title, 'your' addressing the reader and the personal encouragement in the title. Ask: *Do these features draw you to the book?* Explore the Contents page. Ask: *How is it helpful?* (Well-spaced and clear, makes the book seem manageable.) Comment on the author's enthusiasm for football, shown by his early role model. Check that the children know who John Barnes is and that he was a very successful footballer. Question the children on their knowledge of the murder of Stephen Lawrence. Together, discuss question 1 on the bookmark. Emphasise the author's admiration for Stephen and the word 'superhero'. Point out the repetition of the title and discuss the effect of Mandela speaking out: people learned the truth about Stephen. Investigate the author's thoughts about success and why he strives for it: to be 'the best role model' for his son. Point out how he turns attention to the reader with 'your future'. Consider the clear list and explanation of what will follow: nine chapters providing tools for the reader's successful future.

Chapter 1 You Are Your Own Superhero

Comment on Stuart Lawrence's positive attitude, shown by his list of what he is good at (his superpowers). Remind the children that 'unique' means being special. Ask: *Does the author think we should be worried about being different?* Point out his words 'differences are something to celebrate' and his advice to avoid comparing ourselves to others unnecessarily. Emphasise the regular use of 'you'. Ask: *What is the effect?* (The reader feels personal involvement.) Point out the practical activity of writing in a notepad. Let the children try it. Do they find the exercise effective? Ask the children if they have noticed the author's repetition of certain words and phrases to help put his message across. Organise group discussions for question 8 on the bookmark and share results.

Agree on some important words: 'goals', 'goal setting', 'superhero', 'positive', 'self-confidence', 'successful'. Discuss the use of lists in this chapter and in the Introduction. Direct the children to question 6 on the bookmark for group discussion.

Chapter 2 Personality, Passion, Purpose

Read aloud the chapter title. Ask: *Is the alliteration effective? Do the words become memorable?* Discuss question 3 on the bookmark. Point out the explanation page at the beginning of this chapter. Read aloud the chapter's opening paragraph while the children follow and then discuss question 5 on the bookmark. Agree that Stephen is usually mentioned and praised, probably because the author feels strongly influenced by him. Discuss the author's views about personality. Are the children aware of any changes in their personalities this year?

Point out the author's repeated use of a list. Ask: *Do you find the author's honesty encouraging? Why?* (He admits to common faults.) Point out 'characteristics are things you can learn to change'. Suggest that this helps the reader by giving them confidence to overcome weaknesses. Explain the word 'mindset' (your way of thinking). Together discuss question 4 on the bookmark, considering the author's views on failure and personality change. Investigate the contrasting fixed mindset and growth mindset. Ask: *Which mindset does the author want the reader to develop? Why?* Explore the starred list of ways to develop a growth mindset. Ask: *Which piece of advice do you find most helpful?* Use question 11 on the bookmark to discuss 'the buddy system'. Ask: *Does talking to others help you to improve your moral compass?*

Chapter 3 You Are in Control

Remind the children that the author wants to provide a success tool in each chapter. Let partners use question 3 on the bookmark to predict this chapter's tool (self-control). Explore the author's explanation of how he had to learn self-control and the link to

Stephen's death. Examine the definition of self-control that follows and point out the distinction between animals and humans. Ask: *Had you thought of that for yourself? Did you know that teenagers are more impulsive because their brains are still developing?* Discuss the concept of an unhelpful or helpful voice in everyone's head. Ask the children to try the author's exercise of not exercising self-control at first and then imagining going back and changing their behaviour. Ask: *Does the author's advice work? Could you have used self-control?* Investigate the author's advice on screen time. Ask: *What are the arguments against using a mobile phone first thing in the morning and last thing at night?* (It unsettles your brain.) *Which alternative activity in the list would work for you?* Put the children into groups to review this chapter and discuss questions 4 and 7 on the bookmark. Share results.

Chapter 4 What Attitude?

Point out the early sentence 'I wanted to make Stephen proud, because I knew he would want me to be great'. Discuss question 2 on the bookmark, suggesting that Stephen is a major influence on the teaching in this book. Read aloud the author's definition of attitude as a way of thinking, and point out his distinction between good and bad attitude. Ask: *How do you usually use the word 'attitude' – to describe good or bad behaviour?* Comment on the advice given (to pause before making quick decisions). Ask the children to discuss question 11 on the bookmark.

Study the list of ways to build a positive attitude. Ask: *Which idea do you find most helpful? Why?* Talk about the vocabulary used here and the author's repetition of words from previous chapters. Ask the children to pick out three important words that have already recurred frequently. Indicate 'positive', 'unique', 'great', 'superhero'. These words are all essential to the author's aim of helping the reader achieve success.

Investigate the chapter's final section. Ask: *Why is it likely to be important?* (The heading 'Use Your Voice' reinforces the book's title.) *What does the author's motto about hard work mean? Is it helpful?*

Chapter 5 It's Not Failure, It's Unfinished Business

Read aloud the chapter title and refer to the advice in Chapter 2: 'Swap the word 'failing' with 'learning''. Invite the children to discuss question 3 on the bookmark. Ask: *Do you think the author will build on Chapter 2's words? What new point about failure could he make?* Consider the prominence given to the single statement on the chapter's first page. Together discuss question 11 on the bookmark. Examine the effect of Stephen's death on the author: unwise decisions and poor exam results. Comment on the words 'I needed to change my mindset'. Ask: *What was the result?* (He went to a different college, studied a practical course and achieved the results he needed for university.) Point out the important words 'kept on fighting'; 'positive things, instead of negative'; 'Never quit'. Investigate the ways to turn failure into a positive experience. Ask: *Which piece of advice would work best for you? Do you think the advice to speak to others is valuable?*

Explore the children's understanding of 'free will'. Comment on the examples given that are relevant to their age and lives. Discuss question 7 on the bookmark. Point out the repetition of the book's title and the final message beginning 'When failure knocks at your door…'. Invite the children to discuss question 8 on the bookmark.

Chapter 6 Dream Big

Refer to question 8 on the bookmark to discuss the author's repeated style of using a strong message in capital letters on the opening page of a chapter. Ask: *Do you find this device effective?* Suggest that this page sums up what will follow. Point out the comparison between imagination and a magician's hat. Suggest that this is effective because imagination, like a magician's hat, can produce anything. Try out with the children the exercise with the aeroplane and share the varied results.

Read aloud the short paragraph beginning 'We need to learn…'. Tell the children to read it aloud after you. Explain that the author is emphasising the importance and power of imagination. Comment on the advice divided into short-, mid- and long-term steps. Ask: *Is this wise advice? Does it make a goal more achievable?* Investigate the list of ways to keep your imagination working. Ask: *Which way would* you find easy? Are there any that you would find difficult? Which would improve your imagination? Comment on the author's willingness to be honest about his own experience. Ask the children to re-read the information about Martin Cooper and discuss question 9 on the bookmark.

Chapter 7 Take Your Time

Use the first paragraph and questions 2 and 5 on the bookmark to remind the children about the inspiration for the book. Read about the early time divisions and ask the children how much they already knew about obelisks and sundials. Investigate the author's advice for a day planner. Ask: *Do you find the timetable easy to visualise? Would it improve your time management?* Comment on the author's ability to provide clear examples of putting his advice into practice. Together discuss question 4 on the bookmark. Reminding the children of the book's title, point out the author's encouragement to pass on useful information to others, so that they too can manage time well. Ask: *How does he suggest influencing them?* (Gentle suggestions can work.) Comment on the author's frankness, revealing time wasted by a friend. The author praises him for turning his life around but emphasises that he has lost time to achieve some amazing things. Draw attention to the final page in capital letters. Ask: *What do the words stress?* (Once time has gone, you cannot regain it.)

Chapter 8 What Is Wealth?

Draw attention to the familiar format for the start of a chapter: a statement taking up a whole page and summarising the tool the reader will learn about. Ask: *Does it remain an effective device, even by this stage of the book? Why?* (The chapter is always about a new success tool.) Ask the children to read the first three paragraphs. Comment on how often Stephen is referred to and invite the children to discuss question 2 on the bookmark. Investigate the information about the history of money and the author's emphasis on following your passions, not just a high salary. Point out the name 'Lionel Messi'. Ask: *Is it surprising that the author uses him as an example of a high earner?* (No, the author has already revealed his passion for football.)

Investigate the 'Principle of Three' by discussing together question 11 on the bookmark. Read aloud

the powerful message towards the end of the chapter about helping others 'to have their voice heard'. Invite children to read aloud the author's final summary of the chapter. Ask: *Is this helpful? Does it make the teaching clear?* Direct the children to question 9 on the bookmark for discussion.

Chapter 9 Lifelong Learning

Explore the first two paragraphs and use question 1 on the bookmark to discuss how the author learned his biggest lesson. Ask: *Can you answer the question posed about your biggest lesson?* Investigate the author's explanation of different kinds of learning. Ask: *Is it encouraging to learn 'there is a lesson in almost everything'? Why?* (It is a positive message.) Discuss self-learning and encourage the children to share examples from their own experience. Comment on the author's ability to relate to his readers, and ask the children to discuss question 7 on the bookmark. Discuss the hidden curriculum of your school, inviting the children to discuss question 11 on the bookmark. Let them try the exercise on culture, before comparing their answers with the author's examples.

Investigate the distinction between soft and hard skills. Ask: *What soft and hard skills do you have?* Direct the children to the final two paragraphs. Ask: *What two messages come across?* (We learn from other people; lessons are learned everywhere.)

Chapter 10 Before I Go

Comment on the strong statement on the opening page. Suggest that this is the main message that the author wants readers to take from the book. Investigate his ideas for writing things down. Ask: *What ways of recording does he suggest?* (A notepad, journal and mood board are all mentioned.) *Are these notes and thoughts to be seen as final?* (The author suggests revisiting them and being willing to reflect and change your mind.) Point out the advice to 'reawaken your creativity' when your imagination fades. Investigate the list of some of the book's most important tools. Ask: *Which do you think matters most?* Explore the final two paragraphs. Ask: *What does the author mean? Why is speaking to others important?* (Others can also learn and change.) Use group discussion for questions 10 and 12 on the bookmark.

Silence is Not an Option

by Stuart Lawrence

Focus on...
Meaning

1. What tragic event affects the author during his teenage years? How does this change his life?

2. Explain why Stephen is still a major presence in the author's life. How has Stephen continued to help him?

3. Does the chapter title help you to predict and understand the ideas being put forward?

4. Explain the advice being given here and the author's tips for avoiding going wrong in your life.

Focus on...
Organisation

5. What do you notice about the early part of each chapter? Who and what does the author usually mention? Why?

6. Do you think the author's use of lists is an effective writing device? Give an example and explain how it contributes to the text.

Silence is Not an Option

by Stuart Lawrence

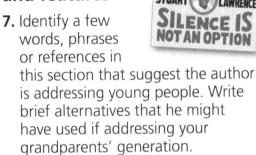

Focus on...
Language and features

7. Identify a few words, phrases or references in this section that suggest the author is addressing young people. Write brief alternatives that he might have used if addressing your grandparents' generation.

8. What devices does the author use to hold our attention and aid our understanding of the message being put across?

Focus on...
Purpose, viewpoints and effects

9. What message are you most aware of here? Does the author want you to admire or criticise the people he mentions? Explain your answer.

10. What is the author's aim in this part of the book? How does he achieve this?

11. Does the author express the only correct opinion here or are there other valid points of view? Support your answer with evidence.

12. How does the author want you to feel about yourself by the end of the book? Give reasons for your opinion.

SHARED READING ▶

Extract 1

- In this section of Chapter 1, the author emphasises that the qualities of politeness and kindness are important for self-confidence and success. Circle 'you' in the first sentence. Ask: *What is the effect of this word effect?* (The reader feels involved.) Let the children re-read the first paragraph. Ask *What is clear about the author's involvement?* Underline the sentence starting 'In my opinion…'. Comment on the writer's frankness. Ask: *Does his honesty make his advice more valuable?*

- Ask: *What examples of kindness are given in the second paragraph?* Encourage the children to re-read the paragraph before sharing answers; underline 'sharing a smile…' to '… a compliment to someone'. Circle 'compliment' and define it simply (saying something nice). Discuss a definition suited to a dictionary, for example, 'an expression of praise'.

- Organise the children into pairs to consider your fluency as you read aloud the second paragraph. Ask: *How did I give the text expression? Did my voice change when I addressed the reader? Did I make the questions effective?*

- Investigate the third paragraph. Point out the personal information that the author reveals about himself. Ask: *What does he realise? What action does he take?* Underline 'Perhaps now…' to '…sacrifices for you'. Ask: *Why is this sentence important?* (It implies that the reader should act as the author did.) Circle 'superheroes', emphasising its importance, as it has already recurred frequently in the book.

- Remind the children of the title of Chapter 1 before they re-read the fourth paragraph. Ask: *Is it an appropriate end to Chapter 1?* (It sums up the message.) *Why has the author made the statement below the final paragraph so noticeable? Are the words made memorable?*

Extract 2

- This extract comes halfway through the book, at the end of Chapter 4 on attitude. Highlight the heading 'Use Your Voice'. Ask: *Are the words similar to another of the author's headings?* Revisit the book title: both headings emphasise the need to speak out.

- Remind the children that this extract closes a chapter. Underline the opening 'So now you know' and comment on its appropriateness as a way of linking this paragraph to what has gone before, pulling the chapter together and bringing it to an end. Re-read the first paragraph. Ask the children to consider what is said. Ask: *Is the emphasis on the reader or the author?* (the reader) Point out how often 'you' is used in this first paragraph and circle examples. Ask: *How is the reader encouraged to act?* (They should communicate with others.)

- Ask: *What immediate change in the writing do you notice in the first sentence of the second paragraph?* Circle 'I' and point out that the author now talks about himself. Circle 'dyslexia' and define it as 'a condition that causes problems with reading, writing and spelling'. Put the children into pairs to read and share responses to the second paragraph. Ask: *What effect did the author's dyslexia have on him? How did he overcome his feeling of failing? How did he gain a positive attitude?* Underline the sentence 'I focused…'. Comment that this sentence sums up how the author developed a positive attitude.

- Underline and read aloud the author's message: 'Hard work beats talent, when talent doesn't work hard.' Ask: *Can you understand the message? Are you inspired by it? Why?*

Extract 3

- Taken from the final chapter, this extract reminds the reader of what they have learned and suggests how to use it. Underline the first sentence. Comment that it emphasises that the book addresses young people. Ask: *Does the author expect you to keep early career dreams?* (Career ideas may change frequently.) Circle 'ambitions' and 'goals'. Ask: *What is noticeable?* (The meanings of the words are similar.)

- Let the children re-read the second paragraph before you explore it together. Ask: *Does the author expect you to remember his advice? What weakness does he recognise?* (You can slip back into old habits.) *What advice do you find helpful?*

- Underline 'By reading…' to '…that potential.' Circle and define 'potential' (what you can do). Circle 'amazing' and 'incredible'. Ask: *How do the adjectives make you feel? Are you inspired and proud?* Let the children listen as you read aloud the two sentences, as if the author is saying them. Point out that your reading tone, volume, speed and emphasis contribute to your reading fluency. Invite the children to read aloud the sentences after you.

- Examine the tools mentioned. Ask: *How are they presented? Why is a list effective?* (The format makes the text seem accessible.) Circle 'self' in the headings. Ask: *Why is it important?* (It reminds the reader to focus on their behaviour.)

- Underline 'thinking about your own feelings and behaviour'. Comment on the simple clarity of the author's definition. Ask: *How does he define self-love?* Underline 'Being kind to yourself'. Circle 'superhero' and 'uniqueness'. Ask: *Is it important that the author uses these words in this final chapter?* Agree that they are major themes in the book.

Extract 4

- This extract from *Wonder*, a novel by RJ Palacio, is about a fictional boy called August whose severe facial deformities have made him afraid of attending school. This is the end of the book when, after a year at school, August realises that others accept and gain from his differences.

- Underline all the names in the first paragraph. Comment on how many there are. Ask: *Will the reader be confused by so many names?* Suggest that such detail is common at the end of a novel, as the characters are familiar by now.

- Investigate the second paragraph. Ask: *What mood does the writer create?* Circle 'perfect', 'happy' and 'hero'. Suggest that these words contribute to a contented mood. Underline the final sentence and circle 'like'. Ask: *What type of comparison does 'like' create?* (a simile). Together, do a choral reading of the passage, trying to match the mood with the way you speak.

- Underline 'giggly kind of mood' and comment on the laughter in the groups and August's awareness of what others are doing and saying. Ask: *Is it sad that Mom is alone?* Underline 'smiling to herself' and 'seemed happy'.

- Circle 'hugging'. Suggest that August has gained strength and self-confidence from being at school. He knows he has his mum to thank for persuading him. Underline 'Thank *you*, Auggie'. Ask: *Is this surprising? What does Mom mean?* (She recognises that August's physical difference does not stop him being a special person. *Which word does she use to confirm this?* ('wonder') *Why is this a fitting end to the book?* (It is also the title.)

Extract 1

Don't you just hate it when you hold the door open for someone and they don't say thank you? As the saying goes, manners cost nothing. In my opinion, manners have helped me more in life than anything else. Good manners make people feel more comfortable around you. You could even say being polite is a superpower!

Beyond being polite, one of the greatest superpowers a person can have is being kind. Even small things, like sharing a smile with someone, offering to help someone with their bags or giving a compliment to someone can go a really long way. These kindnesses can even help to boost other people's self-confidence. What small act of kindness were you once shown that you will never forget? Did it boost your self-confidence?

When people do kind things for us, it's important to say thank you. I was about 22 when I first realized the number of sacrifices my mum had made to help me get to where I wanted to be in life. I picked up the phone and called her to let her know how much I appreciated her and to say thank you. Perhaps now would be a good time for you to find someone who has made sacrifices for you, to let them know you appreciate their help and support. Let's celebrate all the superheroes in our life, who help us become superheroes, too.

You are only ever in competition with yourself. There may be someone else doing, or wanting to do, some of the same things in life, but their purpose or approach may be different. You have something to offer that nobody else can. Be confident in your superpowers and use them to do good things in the world.

Focus on yourself and you will be successful.

Extract 2

Use Your Voice

So now you know the importance and power of your attitude – but don't keep the knowledge to yourself. If you have friends or family members who you feel do not have a positive attitude, or who don't put a lot of effort into things, you can encourage them and give them advice from this book. You never know, the friend or family member you encourage could be the next politician that creates positive change, the next lawyer to fight for someone's freedom or the next life-saving surgeon.

Like most people, I have been through personal challenges. I have dyslexia, and there were times when I wasn't able to complete tasks to my mum's extremely high standards. Even when I became an adult, I still had a feeling of falling short, but I made the decision to build a positive attitude. I focused on what I was good at and accepted what I was not so good at. We are not going to be good at everything and that is okay. I learned that it's not what other people think or say about me that matters, but what I think and say about myself.

If there are any words that I would like you to take away from this chapter, they would be:

Hard work beats talent, when talent doesn't work hard.

When you have a good attitude, that usually means you work hard and hard work can only lead to success.

Extract 3

Over time, your ambitions might change. Right now, you might want to be an architect, but in a year or two, perhaps you'll want to be an interior designer instead. As life goes on, you'll meet new people and learn new things, so it's no wonder some of your goals will change. This is what makes life so exciting!

Use this book every now and then to remind yourself of the powerful tools you've learned. If you find yourself falling back into the habit of wasting time, grab **Silence is Not an Option** and re-read Chapter 7 for motivation and guidance. If you feel your imagination is fading, re-read the Chapter 6 and reawaken your creativity. Look back at the notes you made to reaffirm your passions and your goals.

Your New Tools for Life

By reading this book and self-reflecting, I hope you see that you are amazing. You have incredible potential and I hope that some of the tools in this book will help you achieve that potential. Here's a reminder of just a few of the tools you've been given:

Self-reflection

In each chapter I have asked you to take part in some activities that make you self-reflect, which means thinking about your own feelings and behaviour. Self-reflection helps us to celebrate our strengths and work on our weaknesses.

Self-love

Being kind to yourself is so important! As we talked about in Chapter 1, you are your own superhero. Try to remind yourself of that as often as you can and celebrate your amazing uniqueness.

Self-discipline

Being disciplined will drive you to work hard. Knowing when to turn off the screens and get some work done is a powerful skill.

Extract 4

Extract from *Wonder* by RJ Palacio

We walked to our house for cake and ice cream after the reception. Jack and his parents and his little brother, Jamie. Summer and her mother. Uncle Po and Aunt Kate. Uncle Ben, Tata and Poppa. Justin and Via and Miranda. Mom and Dad.

It was one of those great June days when the sky is completely blue and the sun is shining but it isn't so hot that you wish you were on the beach instead. It was just the perfect day. Everyone was happy. I still felt like I was floating, the *Star Wars* hero music in my head.

I walked with Summer and Jack, and we just couldn't stop cracking up. Everything made us laugh. We were in that giggly kind of mood where all someone has to do is look at you and you start laughing.

I heard Dad's voice up ahead and looked up. He was telling everyone a funny story as they walked down Amesfort Avenue. The grown-ups were all laughing, too. It was like Mom always said: Dad could be a comedian.

I noticed Mom wasn't walking with the group of grown-ups, so I looked behind me. She was hanging back a bit, smiling to herself like she was thinking of something sweet. She seemed happy.

I took a few steps back and surprised her by hugging her as she walked. She put her arm around me and gave me a squeeze.

"Thank you for making me go to school," I said quietly.

She hugged me close and leaned down and kissed the top of my head.

"Thank *you*, Auggie," she answered softly.

"For what?"

"For everything you've given us," she said. "For coming into our lives. For being you."

She bent down and whispered in my ear. "You really are a wonder, Auggie. You are a wonder."

GRAMMAR, PUNCTUATION & SPELLING ▶

1. Different meanings

Objective
To spell and understand homophones and other words that are easily confused.

What you need
Copies of *Silence is Not an Option*, photocopiable page 22 'Different meanings', individual whiteboards.

What to do
- Use this activity after reading Chapter 1. With the children's book copies closed, read aloud the sentence 'Even small things…' to '…really long way.' Emphasise the word 'compliment'. Ask: *What does it mean?* (a polite expression of praise) *Can you spell it?* Let the children write their suggestions on their whiteboards. Invite the children to hold up their whiteboards and look around. Is there a difference of opinion over one letter? Write the correct spelling on your main board and underline the letter 'i'. Explain that using an 'e' here is a common mistake.
- Add 'complement' to the board. Explain that the words are homophones. Ask: *What are homophones? What do you know about their sound, spelling and meaning?* Confirm that homophones sound the same but have different spellings and meanings.
- Write the two meanings, 'a pleasant remark'; 'something that completes', on the board and ask the children to match them to the correct homophone. Demonstrate the use of 'complement' in a sentence: 'Cream is the perfect complement to strawberries.'
- Give out photocopiable page 22 'Different meanings' for the children to match homophones and meanings.

Differentiation
Support: Reduce the number of homophones for children to work on.

Extension: Ask children to write a homophone for each of these words: 'steal', 'mourning', 'assent', 'guest', 'farther'.

2. Writing lists

Objective
To use colons and semicolons correctly when writing lists.

What you need
Copies of *Silence is Not an Option*, photocopiable page 23 'Writing lists'.

What to do
- After reading Chapter 2 write a colon (:) on the whiteboard. Comment that the author frequently uses this punctuation mark. Ask: *What is it?* Let the children, in pairs, search Chapter 2 for examples. Share their results.
- Indicate the colon before the author's 15 characteristics. Re-read 'Get That Growth Mindset Growing' and point out the colon. Ask: *Why are the two colons used?* (They introduce lists.)
- Write a semicolon (;) on the whiteboard. Ask: *What is this punctuation mark called?* Emphasise that this has a very different use from a colon, but may also be connected to a list. Explain that it may separate items in a complicated list.
- Display these two examples: 'Three children have won prizes: Jack, Shami, Jasmine.' 'Prizes are awarded for three subject groups: art, design and technology; maths, science and computing; reading, writing and verbal fluency.' Highlight the colons and semicolons. Explain that the first colon introduces a simple list of names. Ask: *How are the names separated?* Explain that the second colon introduces a complicated list of subject groups. Ask: *How are the three groups separated?* (Semicolons make the divisions clearer.)
- Give out photocopiable page 23 'Writing lists' for the children to add missing colons and semicolons.

Differentiation
Support: Let children work in pairs for the second half of the photocopiable page.

Extension: Ask children to write five sentences of their own using colons and semicolons.

3. Using words

Objective
To understand that words from a text can be useful in their own writing.

What you need
Copies of *Silence is Not an Option*, individual copies of the focus-word table from the online area.

What to do
- After reading Chapter 8, direct the children to its final few pages and point out the words 'vulnerable', 'supportive' and 'impact'. On the whiteboard, write brief explanations for these words in child-friendly language: 'making a big difference', 'could easily suffer', 'helps you out'. Ask: *Which explanation belongs to which focus word?* Confirm the answers.

- Give out the focus-word table for the children to complete the first two columns. Return to the text and read the sentences containing the focus words aloud. Ask: *Could the focus words be used in different sentences?* Share partner and then class ideas before you write the following sentences on the whiteboard: 'Without good health, we are all vulnerable.'; 'Having supportive friends is very important.'; 'You can have a big impact on someone else's life by helping them out when they need it.' Ask the children to copy these sentences into the third column of their chart.

- Ask: *Could the words be useful in contexts other than this book?* List three scenarios: a boy helps his new classmate find his way around; a hard football shot breaks the playground goalpost; a new house is built close to the cliff edge. Organise groups of four to discuss which scenario best allows them to use which focus word. Listen in for interesting sentences to share with the class.

- Finally, provide the children with dictionary definitions to write in column four of the chart.

Differentiation
Support: Let partners collaborate during the group discussion.

Extension: Ask children to write their own sentences using the focus words.

4. Linking words

Objective
To use hyphens to avoid ambiguity.

What you need
Copies of *Silence is Not an Option*, teacher-made worksheet (optional).

What to do
- Complete this activity after finishing the book. Ask questions, encouraging partner discussion before progressing to whole-class exchanges.

- Show a hyphen on the whiteboard. Ask: *What is this punctuation mark? How is it used?* Explain that a hyphen joins two words together to form a new word. Comment that the author often uses hyphens. Ask: *What is Chapter 3 called?* Point out 'problem-solving' in Chapter 3, in the description of the effects of using screens at night. Write the relevant sentence twice on the whiteboard without the hyphen. Underline separately 'problem' and 'solving'. Read aloud the first sentence. Ask: *Did you hear that I left the underlined words separate? Was the sentence's meaning muddled? Was the author's meaning clear?*

- Add the missing hyphen to the second sentence and read it aloud. Ask: *How did my reading change? Did the meaning become clear?* Explain that you linked the two words with a hyphen and the author's meaning became clear. Explain that the hyphen tells the reader to link the words.

- Write these words on the whiteboard or give out your pre-prepared list of words: 'awareness', 'thinking', 'self', 'headed', 'doubt', 'control', 'hearted', 'self', 'ending', 'lasting', 'hot', 'self', 'problem', 'self', 'tempered', 'discipline', 'reflection', 'never', 'self', 'kind', 'self', 'self', 'quick', 'long', 'short', 'never', 'confidence', 'employed', 'solving'. Ask the children to use hyphens to create and write down new linked words from the separate words. They should recognise some of the hyphenated words from *Silence is Not an Option*.

Differentiation
Support: Encourage children to prepare their list of words with a partner.

Extension: Ask children to extend the list of hyphenated words. Suggest checking different reading material.

5. Special endings

Objective

To use the endings '-cial' and '-tial' correctly.

What you need

Copies of *Silence is Not an Option*, photocopiable page 24 'Special endings'.

What to do

- Complete this activity after finishing the book. When posing questions, encourage partner discussion before progressing to whole-class exchanges.

- With the children's books closed, read aloud the second sentence in the section called 'Your New Tools for Life' in Chapter 10. Draw attention to the repeated word 'potential'. Ask: *What does it mean?* (what you are capable of)

- Put the children into pairs and ask them to imagine themselves as English learners who can now speak English well, know the alphabet and its sounds, know the sounds of blended letters, but are not used to spelling correctly. Repeat 'potential' for the children to discuss and say to each other. Suggest partners agree on how they, as English learners, would write it on their individual whiteboards. Share the results. Ask: *Did many of you use 'sh' to create the sound near the end of the word?* Write the correct spelling of 'potential' on the whiteboard.

- Repeat this exercise with 'special', a word that the author often applies to the reader. Ask: *How would a learner spell it?* Write the correct spelling on the whiteboard and underline 'cial'. Explain that it creates the same sound as 'tial'. Talk about how the two spellings are often confused. Explain that there are rules to help: -cial is common after a vowel letter, while -tial is common after a consonant.

- Give out photocopiable page 24 'Special endings' for the children to complete.

Differentiation

Support: In the second half of the activity, ask children to write sentences using six of the words from the top of the sheet.

Extension: Ask the children to also write sentences using less familiar words from the first half of the photocopiable page.

6. Considering possibilities

Objective

To use modal verbs or adverbs to indicate degrees of possibility.

What you need

Copies of *Silence is Not an Option*.

What to do

- Use this activity after finishing the book. Comment that this book often asks the reader to think about what may happen in their future. The author provides a guide to acquiring tools that will help the reader towards a satisfying, successful future. Consequently, the author's words sometimes express degrees of possibility.

- Direct the children to 'Pick Your Passion' in Chapter 2. Point out 'can' and 'might' in the second paragraph. Identify them as modal verbs. Modal verbs are not complete in themselves. They work with a main verb and affect its meaning by indicating the degree of possibility. Ask: *What is the main verb affected by 'can'?* ('push') *What is the verb that 'might' works with?* ('be').

- Explain that modal verbs are used before the main verb and express four areas: possibility, ability, certainty and obligation. Display these modal verbs, but without their category: 'can', 'could' (ability); 'must', 'ought', 'should' (obligation); 'might', 'may' (possibility); 'will', 'would', 'shall' (certainty).

- Write an incomplete passage on the whiteboard for the children to copy and complete using modal verbs: 'At the moment your passion ___ be anything from football to ballet. It doesn't matter. You ___ work at that now. However, the sport ___ not suit you later. You ___ feel differently next year and feel you ___ take up a new hobby. That ___ be fine. The important thing you ___ do is commit yourself to what interests you at the moment. You ___ change your superhero or passion in the future, but you ___ believe in yourself always. Ask: *Can you identify the categories you have used?*

Differentiation

Support: Suggest children work in pairs to prepare their text.

Extension: Let children write another passage containing their unused modal verbs.

Different meanings

- Read each pair of homophones. Look for the correct meaning of each word and write it next to the word in the 'Meanings' column.

an island

made from grain

paper and envelopes

permitted

a metal

basic truth or belief

going down

a gangway between seats

went first

out loud

a first attempt at writing something

a succession of things

disagreement

a current of air

important person

not moving

Homophones	Meanings
1. aisle	1.
2. isle	2.
3. aloud	3.
4. allowed	4.
5. descent	5.
6. dissent	6.
7. draft	7.
8. draught	8.
9. cereal	9.
10. serial	10.
11. led	11.
12. lead	12.
13. stationery	13.
14. stationary	14.
15. principal	15.
16. principle	16.

Writing lists

Remember:

: A colon may be used to **introduce** a list.

; A semicolon may be used **within** a list.

- Add the missing colons and semicolons to these sentences. The punctuation you will need for each sentence is in brackets after the sentence.

1. A person may have three dominant personality characteristics kindness, loyalty and shyness. (Add one colon.)

2. His three siblings can be very different one brother may be ambitious and determined the other brother may be self-confident and very imaginative his sister may be friendly and inquisitive. (Add one colon and two semicolons.)

3. Yet they all possess the three most important qualities being special, being valuable and being unique. (Add one colon.)

4. Fortunately, they all have the same attitude to one another they believe that everyone is remarkable and worth listening to. (Add one colon.)

- Add the missing colons and semicolons to these sentences.

5. A growth mindset lets you develop parts of yourself your character, your intelligence and your talent.

6. A fixed mindset holds you back in many ways it stops you trying new things it makes you give up easily it gives you a negative attitude.

7. Screen time comes in many forms your phone, your games console, your television.

8. All screens have drawbacks they can waste your time they can interrupt your focus they can distract you from your work.

Special endings

- The word endings **-cial** and **-tial** can sound the same.

> If the ending follows a vowel letter, the spelling is usually **-cial**.
>
> If the ending follows a consonant letter, the spelling is usually **-tial**.

- Use the two rules above to add -cial or -tial to complete each word.

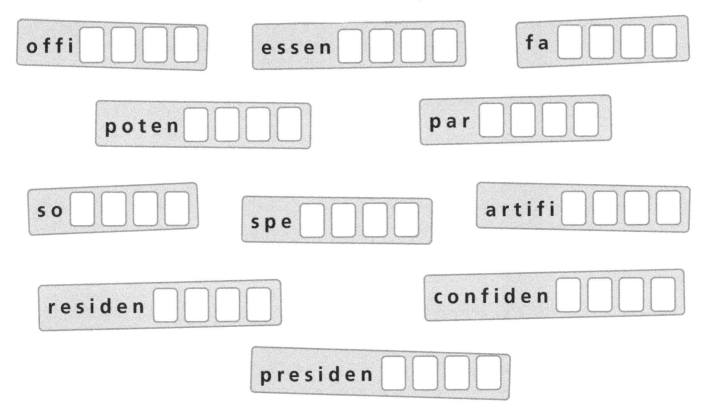

offi ☐☐☐☐   essen ☐☐☐☐   fa ☐☐☐☐

poten ☐☐☐☐   par ☐☐☐☐

so ☐☐☐☐   spe ☐☐☐☐   artifi ☐☐☐☐

residen ☐☐☐☐   confiden ☐☐☐☐

presiden ☐☐☐☐

- The words initial, financial, commercial, provincial, spatial and palatial are exceptions that break the rules above. Write six sentences, each containing one of these words.

1. _____

2. _____

3. _____

4. _____

5. _____

6. _____

CONTENT & STRUCTURE ▶

1. Getting started

Objective
To make comparisons within and across books, to predict what might happen from details stated and implied.

What you need
Copies of *Silence is Not an Option*.

What to do

- Read the Introduction together. When posing questions, encourage partner discussion before individual answers or whole-class exchanges. Ask: *Does the book's title suggest fiction or non-fiction? Why?* (Either seems possible.) Read aloud the Introduction's opening paragraph. Ask: *What is made clear? Is information stated or implied?* Agree that the author states the book's purpose. Suggest fiction would not reveal its story. Conclude that this is non-fiction.

- Point out the continued use of 'I' in the section 'Role Models', and the author's personal family details of his brother's tragic death and his own struggles. Mention his determination to be his own person: 'I want people to get to know me because of the person I am.'

- Explore the author's 'conversation' with the reader. Look at the heading 'Who are you doing it for?' and the questions that follow. Ask: *How do they make you feel? Do they draw you into the book?* Investigate the repeated chapter titles. Ask: *Why is this second list provided? Is it more informative than the Contents page?* Read aloud the final paragraph of the chapter. Ask: *Does 'positivity' seem important? What does the author want by the end of the book?*

- Ask the children to write a paragraph describing the Introduction and how it prepares the reader for what to expect.

Differentiation
Support: Suggest points for the paragraph.
Extension: Expect more writing with textual references.

2. Notepad entries

Objective
To summarise the main ideas drawn from more than one paragraph, identifying key details that support the main idea.

What you need
Copies of *Silence is Not an Option*, photocopiable page 29 'Notepad entries'.

Cross-curricular link
PSHE

What to do

- After reading Chapter 1, refer the children to the Contents page. Comment that the chapters have very different headings, so the concepts involved are likely to vary considerably. Ask: *Are some ideas likely to be new to you? Will there be enough to think about? Could there be too much to remember?*

- Suggest that a written record of what the children read and think as they work through the book could be useful for them in the future. The record should summarise the main teaching and advice in each chapter as well as particular words that the author has brought to the reader's attention.

- Display the headings from photocopiable page 29 'Notepad entries'. Encourage paired discussion as the children apply the headings the Introduction and Chapter 1. Progress to class discussion, reminding the children to relate their answers to the headings displayed. Emphasise to the value of expressing and having confidence in their opinions.

- Give out photocopiable page 29 'Notepad entries' for the children to complete. Suggest using the page and its headings as a template for further writing when they stop at regular stages of the book.

Differentiation
Support: Let partners work together, but encourage a personal reaction to the story.

Extension: Encourage children to use examples from the text to support their opinions.

3. Creating a superhero

Objective
To check that the book makes sense to them, discussing their understanding and exploring the meaning of words in context.

What you need
Copies of *Silence is Not an Option*, photocopiable page 30 'Creating a superhero'.

What to do
- Complete this activity after reading Chapter 1. Encourage partner discussion before inviting individual answers or whole-class exchanges. Point out Chapter 1's title. Ask: *What is a superhero?* (an exceptionally skilful or successful person, often fictional) *Can you think of a fictional superhero?*

- Guide the children in scanning the Introduction. Ask: *Who are the author's heroes?* (John Barnes, Stephen Lawrence, Nelson Mandela) *What reasons does the author have for regarding them as heroes?*

- Read aloud Chapter 1's first paragraph. Ask: *What visual image is painted by the words* 'so I put my cape on'*?* (The author turns himself into a superhero.) Encourage partners to re-read and discuss the early pages of Chapter 1. Ask: *What does the author understand now?* (He must be his own hero.) *What* 'superpowers' *does he realise that he has?* Refer the children to the author's own list of skills at the beginning of Chapter 1.

- Let partners scan the rest of the chapter. Ask: *What does the author keep setting himself?* (goals) *How does he keep thinking?* (positively) *What will thinking positively give a person?* (They will have self-confidence and feel ready to achieve anything.)

- Give out photocopiable page 39 'Creating a superhero' and discuss it. Explain that Stuart Lawrence, the author, is shown in the bottom section of the page; his heroes are in the top section. Invite the children to provide the information for each superhero.

Differentiation
Support: Children work in pairs to prepare their photocopiable pages, before writing independently.

Extension: Ask children to reveal personal superheroes to a partner.

4. A private conversation

Objective
To identify how language, structure and presentation contribute to meaning.

What you need
Copies of *Silence is Not an Option*, photocopiable page 31 'A private conversation'.

What to do
- Use this activity after finishing the book. Encourage partner discussion before progressing to whole-class exchanges. Revisit the first two paragraphs of the Introduction, reminding the children of the author's ambition for this book. Point out 'encourage'. Ask: *Does he do this? Do you feel better about yourself?*

- Progress to Chapter 1. Explain that the author writes in the first person, using 'I' a great deal. Ask: *Which other pronoun is important for a conversation with the reader?* ('you') Read aloud the section beginning 'Now I want to talk…' to '…all the same!' Indicate 'I' and 'you'. Ask: *Which other pronoun is used?* ('we') *Is 'we' effective? Are the reader and author linked?*

- Indicate the instruction that follows. Ask: *Is 'grab' appropriate? Why? Does its informality suit your age group?* Explore the examples on the following page. Ask: *What do 'exams', 'maths' and 'drama' show?* (The author understands the reader's experiences.)

- Suggest that the author recognises how a book such as this could become boring. Ask: *How does he hold the reader's interest?* Mention the activities. Ask: *What is the reader asked to do in Chapters 1 and 2?* (1: answer questions; 2: list personal characteristics).

- Guide the children in scanning Chapter 6. Give out photocopiable page 31 'A private conversation' that identifies ways the author tries to involve the reader in a private conversation. Children should select examples from Chapter 6 that work best for them, describing and quoting the text.

Differentiation
Support: Let partners investigate the text together before writing individual answers.

Extension: Ask children to give more than one example and quote for each statement.

5. Being unique

Objective

To check that the book makes sense to them, exploring the meaning of words in context.

What you need

Copies of *Silence is Not an Option*, dictionaries.

What to do

- After completion of the book, write 'unique' on the whiteboard and define it simply. ('totally different'.) Supply an example sentence: 'My necklace, with its personalised message, is unique'. Invite a volunteer to look up a dictionary definition to add to the whiteboard.

- Point out 'unique' on Chapter 1's first page. Ask: *Why is it given prominence? What does this suggest?* (It is particularly important to the book's message.) After partner and class discussion, ask the children to make a note of its location and an explanation for its choice. Explain that the word is used often in the book. Direct the children to 'Everyone is Unique' in Chapter 2. Guide them in scanning the section. Let partners and then the class discuss the point the author makes and his choice of 'unique'. Ask: *What is he teaching the reader?* Again, the children should write about its location and its selection.

- Read aloud Chapter 6's section on doodling. Ask: *Is 'unique' effective here? Why?* Encourage partners to talk to each other about the point the author is emphasising before they record their thoughts in writing.

- Point out 'unique' after the author's list of cultural expectations in Chapter 9. Ask: *What point is the author making? What is unique?* Follow the discussion with a written record of where and why. Finally, refer the children to Chapter 10's 'Self-love' to discuss and write about this use of 'uniqueness'.

- Let partners compare notes before writing their own paragraph on the author's use of 'unique' and its effect on the reader.

Differentiation

Support: Suggest more partner collaboration before children write their final paragraph.

Extension: Invite children to compile a list of synonyms for 'unique'.

6. Timely advice

Objective

To identify and discuss themes and conventions in writing.

What you need

Copies of *Silence is Not an Option*.

Cross-curricular link

PSHE

What to do

- Use this activity after finishing the book. When posing questions, encourage partner discussion before whole-class exchanges. Comment that time is a recurring theme in the book. Revisit Chapter 3 and the author's warnings about screen time. Ask: *Can you avoid screens taking over your lives? What rules does the author suggest?*

- Remind the children that the author recognises that there can be a right time to act successfully. Re-read the opening paragraph of Chapter 5. Ask: *What did the author do at the wrong time?* (He sat his GCSEs.) *Why should he have waited?* (Stephen had just died and the author needed time to process his feelings.)

- Together scan Chapter 7. Identify 'time management'. Ask: *What does the author mean? Why does he think it is important? What tips does he give for managing time?* Point out the final two sections of Chapter 7. Ask: *What does the author mean by 'there is no turning back time'?* (Wasted time cannot be regained and then used wisely.)

- Direct the children to 'Giving Back' in Chapter 8. Ask: *What does the author encourage? Why is time easy to give?* Let the children read 'Life's Hidden Lessons' in Chapter 9. Ask: *Why is time mentioned? What is the author's advice?*

- Write these headings on the whiteboard, with the chapter numbers in brackets, for the children to copy: Screen time (3); Appropriate time (5); Time management (7); Giving time (8); Being on time (9). Let the children write a brief paragraph for each, explaining the author's advice in their own words.

Differentiation

Support: Use partner discussion to prepare writing. Help children locate time references.

CONTENT & STRUCTURE

7. Constructing the book

Objective
To read books that are structured in different ways and read for a range of purposes.

What you need
Copies of *Silence is Not an Option*, some fiction books with a conventional structure and layout.

What to do

- After reading Chapter 4, remind the children that this is a non-fiction book. Organise them into small groups with copies of *Silence is Not an Option* and some fiction books. Ask: *How is the structure of this book similar to the fiction books? How is its structure different?* Suggest the groups note their observations.

- Invite each group to report brief findings to the class. Agree that both fiction and non-fiction are both usually divided into chapters. Conclude that *Silence is Not an Option* has many different features from most fiction books. Write this list of different features on the whiteboard: headings within a chapter; lists; bullet points; numbers; asterisks; changes in font size; reversal of background and foreground colours.

- Let the children copy the list of features down the middle of a piece of paper, leaving space between them. On the left-hand side of the page, they should write the heading 'Chapter 3'.

- Explain that they will work with a partner to search for and record an example of each listed feature in Chapter 3. Advise them that they will probably not find all of them. Encourage them to use page numbers and quote extracts from the text so that the evidence is easy to find again. Emphasise that they should record just one example of a feature.

- Share and discuss results before the children repeat the exercise, but working individually, for Chapter 4.

Differentiation
Support: Let the children work with a partner for both chapters.

Extension: Expect better observation and understanding of the author's purpose.

8. Stephen's influence

Objective
To provide reasoned justifications for their views

What you need
Copies of *Silence is Not an Option*.

What to do

- After finishing the book, return to the Introduction and point out the author's wish in 'My Brother, Stephen Lawrence' for people to 'like me as Stuart' before they learn of his relationship to Stephen. Similarly, in 'Who are you doing it for?' the author points out his wish to use his own acquired tools to help the reader find success. With the books closed, ask: *Do you remember Stephen being mentioned much in the chapters that followed?*

- Read aloud Chapter 1's first paragraph, as the children follow. Discuss the reference to Stephen's murder and its leading place in the chapter. Ask: *Does the author's memory of his brother help him to gain tools for teaching the reader?* After discussion, let the children write a paragraph about this reference to Stephen, where it comes in the chapter and how it links to what follows.

- Direct the children to Chapter 2's first two paragraphs and read them aloud. Ask: *What do you learn about Stephen? Does the information about Stephen help the author move to addressing the reader in 'Personality and Characteristics'?* After partner and class discussion, ask the children to write a paragraph about this reference to Stephen, its position in the chapter and its influence on what follows.

- Invite the children to work with a partner as they identify three other chapters that begin with a mention of Stephen. For each one, they should discuss the reference before writing a paragraph, giving details of which chapter is involved, what is revealed about Stephen and how this helps the author to address the reader.

Differentiation
Support: Suggest chapters and guide partner discussion.

Notepad entries

- Make notes to help you keep track of what you have read in *Silence is Not an Option.*

Date: ___ / ___ / ___

Where I have stopped: _____
_____

What has been mentioned since my last entry: _____
_____

Important learning: _____
_____

Notable vocabulary and tools: _____
_____

The author's examples: _____
_____

The reader's lessons: _____
_____

What is the book's style? _____
_____

Star rating: ☆ ☆ ☆ ☆ ☆

(Colour in the number of stars you think the book deserves at this stage of your reading.)

My reaction to the book so far: _____
_____

What I think the next chapter will be like: _____
_____

Creating a superhero

- Identify Stuart Lawrence and his three heroes. Write on the lines to provide the special information about each person.

Who? _____

_____

Why? _____

_____

_____

Special skills: _____

_____

_____

_____

Who? _____

_____

Why? _____

_____

_____

Special skills: _____

_____

_____

_____

Who? _____

_____

Why? _____

_____

_____

Special skills: _____

_____

_____

_____

Who? _____

_____

_____

Why? _____

_____

_____

_____

Special skills: _____

_____

_____

_____

Goals _____

_____

_____

_____

A private conversation

- Read each statement. Then give an example from Chapter 6 and support it with a quote from the text.

- The author trusts me with details of his past.

_____

_____

- He keeps turning his attention to me.

_____

_____

- He shows that he understands me and what I say and do.

_____

_____

- He thinks of interesting examples.

_____

_____

- He gives me something to do.

_____

_____

- He tells me a message to remember.

_____

_____

- I think his communication skills are as high as…

1 2 3 4 5 6 7 8 9 10

(Circle the highest mark you would award the author for his ability to communicate with you.)

TALK ABOUT IT ▶

1. A kind story

Objective
To give well-structured narratives for different purposes, including for expressing feelings.

What you need
Copies of *Silence is Not an Option*, photocopiable page 35 'A kind story'.

Cross-curricular link
Drama

What to do
- After reading Chapter 1, leave the children's copies of the book closed. Fluently and clearly, read aloud the author's story about his mother's kindness; his slow recognition; his feelings; his actions; the phone call. Comment that your pauses, intonation (voice's rise and fall), speed and emphasis contribute to your fluency and let them 'hear' the author's sincerity.

- Ask the children to open their book copies and refer them to the relevant section ('Being Polite, Being Kind'). Point out this question: 'What small act of kindness were you once shown that you will never forget?' Give the children a personal example: 'I had a puncture after dark one evening. A colleague waited with me until the breakdown service came.' Ask: *Can you think of a time when someone was kind to you at school or at home? Did another parent give you a lift? Was it related to starting something new?* Let the children consider before they talk to a partner.

- Give them photocopiable page 35 'A kind story' and ask them to make notes and sketches to remind them of the events in their story. Emphasise that they will be telling, not reading, their story, so voice, eye contact and body language will be important. Let the children practise their storytelling first to partners and then in groups.

Differentiation
Support: Encourage pictorial cues and one-word notes on a reduced number of cards.

2. Fixed or growth?

Objective
To participate in discussions and debates.

What you need
Copies of *Silence is Not an Option*, photocopiable page 36 'Fixed or growth?', highlighters.

What to do
- Use this activity after reading Chapter 2. When posing questions, encourage partner discussion before whole-class exchanges. Refer the children to the section on mindset in Chapter 2. Ask: *What does 'mindset' mean?* Point out the author's definition ('way of thinking'). Ask: *What are the two types of mindset?* (fixed and growth) *Which type allows your character, intelligence and talents to develop?* (growth)

- Read aloud the author's final example of a fixed mindset: 'I am either good at it or I'm not'. Suggest that many of us fall into this way of thinking. Compare the final example of a growth mindset. Ask: *Is this a more positive attitude?*

- Give out photocopiable page 36 'Fixed or growth?'. Explain that there are two possible responses to each situation. Challenge the children to identify and colour each response which shows a growth mindset. For the final situations, they must write their own responses.

- Organise the children into pairs to justify their decisions to each other, speaking in sentences and using statement stems, for example, 'I think that…'; 'In my opinion…'; 'I believe that …'.

- Form larger discussion groups, with children taking turns to lead the discussion and justify their choices. Ask: *Do all the new sentences show a growth mindset?*

Differentiation
Support: Let children work with a partner and take turns to read statements aloud to each other.

3. Think for yourself

Objective
To use spoken language to develop understanding through speculating, hypothesising, imagining and exploring ideas.

What you need
Copies of *Silence is Not an Option*.

Cross-curricular link
PSHE

What to do

- After reading Chapter 4, direct the children to the section 'A Positive Attitude Creates Positive Results'. Ask: *What is the author's message?* (People should believe in themselves.) Remind the children of the author's image of a 'little voice inside your head' saying negative thoughts and leading you to the wrong attitude.

- Present a scenario: a new drama club is opening. You have never tried drama, but are interested and thinking of joining. Divide the class into two groups: Group A represents your positive side, ready to believe in yourself and to enjoy the new activity. Group B represents your negative side, worried about failure and concerned it will be too hard. Ask Group A to think of comments to encourage you to join the new class and Group B to think of comments to discourage you.

- Organise the two groups into parallel lines, standing and facing each other. In the role of the pupil trying to make a decision, walk down the 'alley' between the lines. Nod to nearby children to speak their comments. At the end of the alley, having heard their voices, make your decision: go to drama club or stay away. Choose children to be the pupil making their decision and repeat the conscience alley. What decision does each person make?

- Try the activity where the author gives advice about limiting screen time and suggests ways to create a positive attitude (near the end of Chapter 4). Group A must appeal to the children's responsible side to take a break from screens. Group B must encourage screen use.

Differentiation
Support: Let children share comments with a partner.

4. Taking advice

Objective
To take part in role play.

What you need
Copies of *Silence is Not an Option*.

Cross-curricular link
PSHE

What to do

- After reading Chapter 5, return to the beginning of the chapter and re-read the first two paragraphs. Ask: *What life mistake did the author make? Why do you think he decided to take his exams that year after such a tragedy?* Agree that he probably thought it was what his brother would have wanted and that he possibly found it hard to think clearly. Certainly, the author did not give himself time to think.

- Suggest the author needed to give himself time to talk to others and take advice. Ask: *Who would have been the best people to consult?* Agree that he needed to talk to people who knew him and understood what taking exams or leaving them for a year involved. Share ideas and write these suggestions on the whiteboard: friends; teachers; members of his wider family or community; older students.

- Ask the children, in pairs, to take the parts of two of Stuart's teachers, talking in role to each other about whether Stuart should delay his exams for a year. After two minutes, stop the improvised conversations, but leave one pair in role. Invite others to question them.

- Hold similar paired conversations between: students in Stuart's year at school or the year above; two adult members of his wider family or community; his head teacher and deputy head. Each time, invite children to question the pairs left in role. Ask: *What have you decided about what you have heard? Would Stuart have been offered different advice?*

Differentiation
Support: Provide the children with sentence stems for dialogue openers.

Extension: Expect greater thought about the disadvantages and advantages of postponing the exams.

5. Speak up

Objective
To participate in discussions and debates.

What you need
Copies of *Silence is Not an Option*, photocopiable page 36 'Speak up'.

What to do
- After finishing the book, comment that the author often criticises people's use of screens. Ask: *What screens does he mean? Is he including phones?*

- Revisit Chapter 3 and together scan the section 'Screen Time'. Ask: *How does blue light affect sleep? Is it wise to use a phone in the hour before going to bed?* (Phones make us alert, so getting to sleep is more difficult.) Extend the topic, with the children answering a partner before you accept individual answers. Ask: *Do you have a mobile phone? Do you plan to have one? Is it tempting to check your phone very frequently?*

- Discuss your school's policy on phones. Comment that some schools, usually secondary, allow pupils to keep phones all day; other schools lock them in a safe place until home-time. Suggest that this would be an interesting topic for debate, as there are probably different views in the class. Ask the children to pick a side: keep the phone on you or hand it in. Give out photocopiable page 37 'Speak up'. Let partners on the same side discuss the statements, cut them out and select the ones to support their case. Explain that some statements are useful for supporting either side. Invite the children to write up to three new supporting arguments on the blank cards.

- Chair a class debate, listening to arguments from both sides. Encourage everyone to speak, and remind them to open their sentences with sentence stems, for example: 'In my opinion…', 'I think that…'. Hold a final vote.

Differentiation
Support: Let children read out one of their supporting statements.

Extension: Ask for arguments for a compromise, such as only having phones at break.

6. Managing time

Objective
To consider and evaluate different viewpoints, attending to and building on the contribution of others.

What you need
Copies of *Silence is Not an Option*.

What to do
- Use this activity after completing the book. Refer the children to Chapter 7. Remind them of the author's emphasis on efficient time management. Ask: *What practical idea does he have for planning your time?* Point out his list of suggestions linked to making a timetable.

- Ask partners to share information about what they do in the hours between finishing school and before bedtime. Ask: *Do you fit everything in? Is there something you never seem to have time for?* Write some common activities on the whiteboard: homework, sport, reading, meeting a friend.

- Ask the children to make their own timetable for a typical evening. Divide the children into discussion groups of about four to compare timetables. Ask: *Are some people fitting more into their evening? Has someone made particularly wise use of their time?* Emphasise the need to listen to one another and to be ready to consider and alter their opinion on their own time management. Ask: *Is there anything the whole group agrees on?* Suggest that they make a written note of any important points.

- During the discussions, move among the groups and encourage the children to listen politely and to evaluate and build on a viewpoint with their contribution. Invite a spokesperson from each group to sum up their group's feelings about how they manage their time and the ways they have decided to improve it. Let everyone make an alternative timetable. Ask: *Does it look better? What changes have you made?*

Differentiation
Support: Model giving an opinion, or opening the discussion, using a sentence stem.

Extension: Encourage children to respond to the viewpoint of others.

A kind story

- Write notes and draw sketches to complete these cards.
  Then use them to help you tell your story.

Explaining the situation
Where were you?
What were you doing?

Something went wrong
What happened?
How did you feel?

The act of kindness
Who helped you?
What did they do?

Afterwards
How did you express your
gratitude?

How you behaved
at the time
Did you immediately recognise their great kindness?
Did you forget to thank
them properly?

Fixed or growth?

- Read the text, in bold, about each situation.

- Highlight the response that shows a growth mindset.

> **A new Spanish class is starting after school.**
>
> I stick to what I know.
>
> I like trying new things.

> **The coach says I need to work on my shooting skills.**
>
> Feedback will help me to improve.
>
> I hate being criticised.

> **Learning to ride a bike is taking me ages.**
>
> I think I'll give up cycling.
>
> I'll just have to try harder.

> **The book I've chosen is longer than I realised.**
>
> It'll take a while to finish, but it will be worth it.
>
> I'll swap it for a shorter one.

> **I got six spellings wrong in the test.**
>
> I'm useless at spelling.
>
> That's 14 correct ones. I'm nearly there!

> **I can choose hockey or basketball next term.**
>
> I had better choose the one I know I can do.
>
> Choosing a new sport will be an exciting challenge.

Write your own responses for these situations. Remember to think of a response to show a fixed mindset and another to show a growth mindset.

- My year will be sorted into three new classes.

_____

_____

- We are no longer allowed to bring phones to school.

_____

_____

Speak up

- Cut out all the statements.
- Do you want pupils to keep their phones with them in school or hand them in? Choose the statements that support your case.

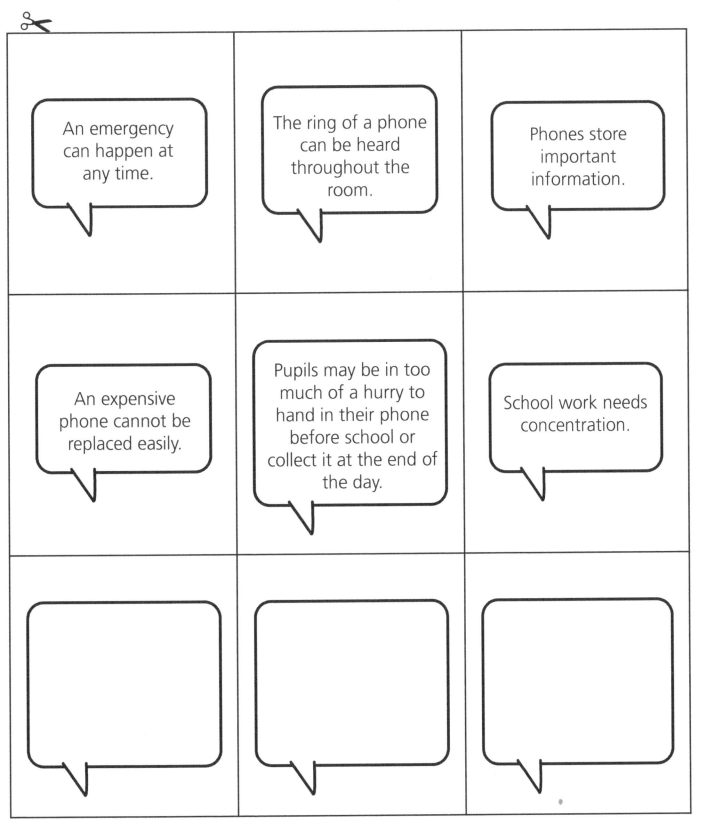

An emergency can happen at any time.

The ring of a phone can be heard throughout the room.

Phones store important information.

An expensive phone cannot be replaced easily.

Pupils may be in too much of a hurry to hand in their phone before school or collect it at the end of the day.

School work needs concentration.

GET WRITING ▶

1. Making space

> ### Objective
> To draft and write by précising longer passages.
>
> ### What you need
> Copies of *Silence is Not an Option*, access to computers.

What to do

- After reading Chapter 1, comment that writers often need to reduce part of a book. Introduce the word 'précis' (a shorter version of a text). If text takes up too much space, yet writers want to retain that part, they can write a précis, or summary, of it.

- Put the children into pairs and hold partner discussions about what a précis should include. Widen this to a class discussion. Agree that main points will be kept, but may be reworded; unnecessary detail and repetition will be omitted.

- Direct the children to the first three paragraphs of 'Being Polite, Being Kind' in Chapter 1. Explain that the word count is about 234 words; the author wants to reduce it to no more than 170 words. Together, explore the three paragraphs. Share ideas on what should be kept: why good manners and politeness are important; some examples; the story about the author's mother; the word 'superpower'. Ask: *What could be omitted?* Suggest that any repetition is removed, and some detail could be omitted from the phone call description in the third paragraph.

- Encourage the children to makes notes before they use computers to type their rough draft and final précis.

> ### Differentiation
> **Support:** Let children do a draft précis with a partner before typing their own.
>
> **Extension:** Ask children to précis the first three paragraphs under 'Privilege' in Chapter 1.

2. Stay positive

> ### Objective
> To note and develop initial ideas, drawing on reading and research where necessary.
>
> ### What you need
> Copies of *Silence is Not an Option*.

What to do

- Use this activity after finishing Chapter 4. When asking questions, let partners answer each other before you widen the discussion. Emphasise the importance of this chapter's tool. Ask: *Why is a positive attitude important? What does it allow us to do?* (believe in ourselves, try new things and find success) Ask: *What is the result of a negative attitude?* (It holds us back and stops us achieving our potential.)

- Refer the children to 'Build That Positive Attitude' in Chapter 4. Read aloud the list of ideas as the children follow. Ask: *Which do you find most helpful? Can you think of others to add?* After partner discussion, share ideas for additions to the book's list. Write some on the whiteboard: 'Try something new'; 'Practise something difficult every day'; 'Count your wise decisions'; 'Offer advice to others'; 'Keep a success journal'.

- Explain that you want the children to write three new ways to build a positive attitude to add to the author's list. The children may choose from the whiteboard or think of their own. For each, they should follow the style of the ones in the book. Suggest the children make notes before writing their final versions.

> ### Differentiation
> **Support:** Encourage preliminary partner preparation and accept two new ways.

3. Chapter 9 and a half

Objective
To plan by identifying the purpose of the writing.

What you need
Copies of *Silence is Not an Option*, photocopiable page 41 'Chapter 9 and a half'.

What to do

- Complete this activity after reading Chapter 9. When asking questions let partners discuss their thoughts before you accept answers from the class. Explain that authors sometimes make changes to their original books, perhaps in a later reprint. Direct the children to the Introduction. Ask: *How many tools are listed?* (nine) *Would ten have been a more satisfactory round number?*

- Set the scenario: the author has decided to write another chapter about a different, tenth tool. It will be placed between the present Chapters 9 and 10. Share ideas about what the new tool could be. Suggest that the author has not yet chosen the chapter title, but wants the chapter to be about making your voice heard. Ask: *What title would you choose?*

- The new chapter should follow the style of other chapters with: an interesting title; headings dividing the sections; examples of what to do; a notepad activity for the reader; a list with the items marked clearly; a memorable, distinctive message.

- Give out photocopiable page 42 'Chapter 9 and a half' and tell the children to imagine that they are the author using this page to plan their chapter. Remind them that they will write notes, not sentences, and that they may want to add planning bubbles. Keep the children's chapter plans for a future writing session.

Differentiation

Support: Suggest the children exchange ideas with a partner before writing their plan.

Extension: Expect the children to plan imaginatively.

4. Extra pages

Objective
To select the appropriate form and use other similar writing as models for their own.

What you need
Copies of *Silence is Not an Option*, the children's completed page 'Chapter 9 and a half'.

What to do

- Do this activity after finishing Chapter 9 and completing the previous activity 'Chapter 9 and a half'. Refer the children to the two final sections of Chapter 9. Read aloud the sections as the children follow. Point out the writer's use of present tense verbs, for example, 'come' and 'know'; his personal involvement in the text, for example, 'I, a former teacher'; the way he addresses 'you', the reader; his accurate and varied punctuation with a dash, exclamation mark and semicolon all chosen within two paragraphs.

- Remind the children that they have planned an additional chapter which will introduce a new tool. Emphasise that it is important that it matches the writing style of previous chapters.

- Read aloud the final paragraph again. Draw attention to the final sentence. Ask the children to explain it to a partner. Agree that it encourages the reader to pass on their new knowledge and skills. Point out the words 'Speak up'. Ask: *Do these words lead smoothly to the new chapter you have planned?*

- Return the children's completed photocopiable page 41 'Chapter 9 and a half' and encourage them to remind themselves of what they planned, perhaps by explaining their notes to a partner. Use an extended writing session for the children to write the new chapter. Remind them to use mainly the present tense and to follow the author's style and layout.

Differentiation

Support: Let partners spend longer explaining their notes to each other before writing.

Extension: Expect children to follow the book's style more closely.

5. Achieving goals

Objectives

To plan their writing by noting and developing initial ideas, drawing on reading and research where necessary.

What you need

Copies of *Silence is Not an Option*, photocopiable page 42 'Achieving goals'.

Cross-curricular link

PSHE

What to do

- After reading Chapter 10, put the children into pairs. Let partners exchange answers to your questions before individual answers or whole-class discussion. Refer the children to the chapter's opening page. Ask: *What does the author suggest starting?* (a journal) *What would be the purpose?* (to plan goals and monitor attitude)

- Read aloud to the children the first paragraph of 'The Power of Your Notepad'. Comment on the references to 'a mood board' and 'inspirational quotes'. Ask: *How could these ideas help you?* Suggest that they will identify where you could be losing focus and which tools need revision. Consider the mention of a mood board. Ask: *Why is understanding your mood important?* (You will identify which of the tools you are not using and if your attitude is wrong.)

- Remind the children of words that the author finds inspiring and quotes in Chapter 8: 'The most important project you will ever work on will be yourself'. Suggest that many of the author's own words are memorable and inspiring. Point out 'Hard work beats talent, when talent doesn't work hard' in Chapter 4 and 'Focus on yourself and you will be successful' in Chapter 1.

- Give out photocopiable page 42 'Achieving goals'. Invite the children to think about a recent day or a few days when they were trying to achieve something. Suggest making notes before completing the page in sentences.

Differentiation

Support: Let children discuss and make notes with a partner.

Extension: Challenge children to think of the steps they need to take to achieve their goal.

6. Recommending books

Objective

To assess the effectiveness of their own and others' writing.

What you need

Copies of *Silence is Not an Option*, photocopiable page 43 'Recommending books'.

What to do

- Use this activity after finishing the book. Ask the children if they have ever watched someone choosing a book from an online bookshop. Ask: *How did the buyer make their choice? Did they read any of the reviews?* Explain that reviews are written by someone who has already read the book. Suggest that book reviews can be a reliable guide for a buyer. Ask: *What would the buyer want and not want in a review? How should the review help?* Share ideas, concluding that the buyer needs enough information to work out if the book will suit them.

- Ask: *What is written in a book review?* Share ideas as a class on important information to include: title; author; what the book is about; style; personal opinion; its suitability for others.

- Put the children into discussion groups to talk about *Silence is Not an Option*. Ask: *What did you find effective about the book? Which ideas worked best for you? Which age group would benefit?*

- Explain that you want to recommend this book to other teachers of your class's age group. Book reviews from children the same age as their own pupils will be particularly helpful when teachers are deciding whether to choose it.

- Give out photocopiable page 43 'Recommending books' and invite the children to write a personal review of *Silence is Not an Option*. Ask them to write full sentences in most sections.

Differentiation

Support: Encourage partner discussion when children are deciding what they most liked or disliked, and the reader it would suit.

Extension: Invite children to write a review of a different book they have enjoyed recently.

Chapter 9 and a half

- Note your ideas for the new chapter in each of the boxes.

Title of new chapter
Make it about speaking up.

_____
_____

Explanation of what this tool means
Explain the importance of setting goals and speaking up when necessary.

_____
_____
_____

A practical activity for the reader
Will the reader use a notepad?

_____
_____
_____

What people often find difficult with this tool
Suggest ways to feel more confident about giving an opinion.

_____
_____
_____

How to improve
Give advice so that others respect what you say.

_____
_____
_____
_____

Heroes to look up to
Think of a famous person, a family member or friend who has spoken up about an important issue.

_____
_____
_____

Inspirational words
Think of a strong, memorable sentence.

_____
_____
_____

Achieving goals

- Think about a goal you have set yourself recently.
- Complete this page of your journal.

Day: _____   Date: __ /__ /____

What was my goal?_____

_____

_____

Which of my tools did I most need?_____

_____

_____

What was my mood?_____

_____

_____

Which words could inspire me?_____

_____

_____

How did I get on?_____

_____

_____

Which chapter will help me now?_____

_____

Recommending books

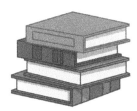

• Use this page to help you write a review of *Silence is Not an Option*.

Title:

Author:

About the content:

Special features:

The part that most inspired me:

The part that least inspired me:

Who would benefit from this book?

Star rating: ☆☆☆☆☆

ASSESSMENT ▶

1. Clear messages

> **Objective**
> To identify how language, structure and presentation contribute to meaning.
>
> **What you need**
> Copies of *Silence is Not an Option*.

What to do

- After reading Chapter 4, explore its message. Let partners exchange answers before class discussion. Ask: *What tool does this chapter teach? How does the teaching succeed?* Suggest that the author communicates his message successfully through language, structure and presentation. Explain that 'language' refers to his words; 'structure' is how text is organised and fits together; 'presentation' is the text's appearance.

- Write the three words and their definitions on the whiteboard. Ask: *Which chapter words most affect you? Why?* Point out 'positive', 'power', 'focused' and 'success'. Invite the children to write Chapter 4's title, the heading 'Language', and a paragraph about how language helps the chapter's message, quoting words that they find effective.

- Scan Chapter 4's structure. Point out the question title; the explanation of 'attitude'; the examples of both positive and negative attitude. Ask: *Do the parts fit together?* Tell the children to add the heading 'Structure' and write about how the chapter's structure makes the author's message clear.

- Refer to sample pages from the chapter. Ask: *What do you notice?* Select some presentational features, for example: bold font, headings, bullet points. Invite the children to write a paragraph about the presentation in this chapter, referring to how and where it is effective.

> **Differentiation**
> **Support:** Accept one or two references to the text.
>
> **Extension:** Challenge children to include more textual references.

2. Using facts

> **Objective**
> To distinguish between statements of fact and opinion.
>
> **What you need**
> Copies of *Silence is Not an Option*.

What to do

- After finishing Chapter 7, return to the section 'Using your notepad'. Read aloud the sentence 'Sure you could watch TV…'. Point out 'mess around'. Ask: *Are the words disapproving?* Compare these words with the approving 'more productive'. Ask: *Does the author express a preference for using a screen or doing something else?* (doing something else)

- Comment that although the author does not condemn screen activities, he does warn against spending too much time on them. Ask: *What does the author think about mobile phones? How do you know this? Does he have facts to back up his opinion?* Encourage partner discussion, as the children search Chapters 4 and 6 for references to screens, and make notes. Share the results, distinguishing between statements of fact and opinion.

- Suggest that the author could have given advice about screens in a pull-out section in the book. This section would need to be set out well to appeal to readers of the children's age and hold their attention. Clear facts would be useful to back up the author's opinion and to persuade the reader. Ask the children to plan this pull-out section before writing it.

> **Differentiation**
> **Support:** Let partners make notes together before writing independently. When editing, partners could advise each other on presentation and separating facts from opinion.
>
> **Extension:** Encourage children to make a clear distinction between facts and opinion in their writing.

3. Detective work

Objective
To retrieve, record and present information from non-fiction.

What you need
Copies of *Silence is Not an Option*, photocopiable page 47 'Detective work'.

What to do
- Complete this activity after finishing the book. When posing oral questions, encourage partner discussion before progressing to whole-class exchanges.

- Display subject non-fiction books that the children are familiar with, for example, a science or geography book. Read aloud an extract from one of them. Ask: *What is mentioned?* (the subject in that section) *Is the book written in the first or third person? Is the author's personal story linked to the science teaching?* Agree that 'I' is unlikely to be used and the reader is unlikely to learn about the author.

- Suggest that *Silence is Not an Option* is an unusual non-fiction book because the author does not just teach his subject. He also writes in the first person and divulges a considerable amount of information about himself.

- Let partners consult each other as they see how much they can remember about the author. Ask: *Why was John Barnes his early hero?* (He was a popular, successful footballer.) *What personal reading and writing problem does the author have?* (dyslexia) *What is the name of the author's son?* (Theo) *How old is his son?* (10) *What college course did the author do instead of his GCSEs?* (BTEC) Point out that this information is revealed almost casually as the author teaches the reader about the tools needed for a successful life.

- Give out photocopiable page 47 'Detective work'. The children should work independently as they search Chapters 8, 9 and 'About the author' to answer the questions. Challenge them to provide a written answer for each question.

Differentiation
Support: Guide children to the relevant chapters and expect simpler answers.

Extension: Invite children to write three other questions for these sections.

4. Self-reflection

Objective
To use further organisational and presentational devices to structure text and to guide the reader.

What you need
Copies of *Silence is Not an Option*.

What to do
- After finishing the book, refer the children to the opening paragraph of Chapter 10 and read it aloud. Encourage partner answers to your questions before progressing to class discussion. Ask: *Has the book achieved its purpose? Has it changed you? Are you more confident about the future?*

- Refer the children to the nine tools listed in the Contents and, with more detail, in the Introduction. Ask: *Which three tools did you most lack before? Do you understand them more now? How will you use them in the future?* Encourage the children to justify their answers.

- Explain that you want the children to do a piece of non-fiction writing about their relationship with this book and how it has changed them. Share ideas on how to set out the writing. Talk about headings, bullet points and underlining. Consider dividing their writing into sections: an introduction in which they name the three tools from the author's list that they had the most to learn about; a section about their past actions; a section about their present understanding of how to apply these three tools; a section about future changes that they hope to make. Emphasise that the children can choose how to set out their writing.

- Remind the children that they will be changing verb tense as they move between past, present and future, so they will need to check their verb tenses carefully. Allow time for the children to write a rough draft before their final piece.

Differentiation
Support: Let partners advise each other on their drafts before writing independently.

Extension: Let children select a fourth tool.

5. Dear Stuart...

Objective
To select appropriate grammar and vocabulary, understanding how such choices can change and enhance meaning.

What you need
Copies of *Silence is Not an Option*, access to computers.

What to do
- Complete this activity after finishing the book. Encourage partner exchanges in response to questions before progressing to class discussion. Read aloud the book title to the children. Ask: *What did you think this book was about on first reading the title? Were you right? Would you have chosen it?* Share ideas.

- Comment that selecting words for the title is a major decision as the title must attract the reader. Suggest that the author may have struggled to reach a final decision on the wording for the title. Ask: *Who would probably offer advice?* (the editor)

- Ask the children to imagine themselves as an editor and give them the following scenario: You (the editor) like the title of the book, but you are concerned that its meaning is unclear. You want a new title and must write to the author about it. Point out that the relationship between editor and author must be a strong one, so the letter's language is important. Emphasise the need to establish a friendly tone, so that the relationship between you and the author remains a happy one.

- Propose writing the letter in this way: a paragraph saying what you like about this title; a paragraph saying why you think it could be even better; a paragraph putting forward and justifying your suggestion. Put the plan on the whiteboard.

- Encourage the children to write a draft version of their letter before typing a final version. Keep the finished letters for a future activity.

Differentiation
Support: When editing draft versions, partners could advise each other on words and phrases.

Extension: Challenge children to think of more than one suggestion, using carefully chosen vocabulary.

6. Just to be clear...

Objective
To perform their own compositions, using appropriate intonation, volume and movement so that meaning is clear.

What you need
Copies of *Silence is Not an Option*.

What to do
- Use this activity after finishing the book and completing the previous activity 'Dear Stuart...'. When posing the questions suggested here, ask partners to exchange answers before progressing to whole-class exchanges. Remind the children of their finished work in 'Dear Stuart...'. Explain that they took the role of editor and wrote to the author. Ask: *What was the letter about?* (the title of this book) *What did the editor want to achieve?* (changing the title) *What was the editor trying to avoid?* (offending the author)

- Organise the children into pairs (different pairs from the previous activity) to examine and discuss each other's letters. Ask: *Which words would they pick out as friendly? Which grammatical constructions could sound formal?* Suggest that tone is not always obvious when read; voice and body language have to do some of the work too.

- Ask the children to practise reading their letters to themselves and then to their partner (the author). When reading, the 'editor' must be careful to use the appropriate tone of voice, intonation and volume so that a friendly mood is clear. Explain that relaxed body language and a smiling face will establish a positive attitude towards the book and its title; this is followed by a friendly suggestion to make the title even better.

- Let partners score each other's reading performance out of ten. Move among the children so that you can make your own assessments and recognise the link between written language and reading fluency.

Differentiation
Extension: Invite confident readers to read their letters to the class.

Detective work

- Search Chapters 8 and 9 and the 'About the author' section to find the answers to these questions.

What has the author taken a sports course in?

_____

_____

What does the author try not to waste?

_____

_____

What is the author's culture?

_____

_____

What nationality was the author's great-aunt?

_____

_____

What did she pass on to the author?

_____

_____

What job did the author do for 15 years?

_____

_____

What is the author's work now?

_____

_____

Why is 22 April important to the author?

_____

_____

SCHOLASTIC

READ & RESPOND

Available in this series:

978-1407-15879-2

978-1407-14224-1

978-1407-16063-4

978-1407-16056-6

978-1407-14228-9

978-1407-16069-6

978-1407-16070-2

978-1407-16071-9

978-1407-14230-2

978-1407-16057-3

978-1407-16064-1

978-1407-14223-4

978-0702-30890-1

978-0702-30859-8

To find out more,
visit www.scholastic.co.uk/read-and-respond